19th Century Innovations
Paving the Way

Matthew McArdle

Consultants

Vanessa Ann Gunther, Ph.D.
Department of History
Chapman University

Nicholas Baker, Ed.D.
Supervisor of Curriculum and Instruction
Colonial School District, DE

Katie Blomquist, Ed.S.
Fairfax County Public Schools

Publishing Credits

Rachelle Cracchiolo, M.S.Ed., *Publisher*
Conni Medina, M.A.Ed., *Managing Editor*
Emily R. Smith, M.A.Ed., *Series Developer*
Diana Kenney, M.A.Ed., NBCT, *Content Director*
Courtney Patterson, *Senior Graphic Designer*
Lynette Ordoñez, *Editor*

Image Credits: pp. 2, 5, 8 (top), 14, 23, 24, 25 Sarin Images/Granger, NYC; pp. 4, 14, 16, 17 North Wind Picture Archives; pp. 7 (top), 9, 19 Granger, NYC; pp. 7 (bottom), 10, 16 New York Public Library Digital Collections; p.8 (botttom) LOC [LC_HAER-IND-2-NEHA-V-1]; p. 11 LOC [LC-DIG-pga-07482]; pp. 15, 20, 21 Peter Newark American Pictures/Bridgeman Images; p. 22 LOC [LC-DIG-ppmsca-38401]; p. 23 LOC [2014636842]; p. 24 Wikimedia Commons/Public Domain; p. 26 LOC [LC-DIG-ds-02423]; pp. 26, 32, back cover SSPL/Getty Images; all other images from iStock and/or Shutterstock.

Library of Congress Cataloging-in-Publication Data

Names: McArdle, Matthew.
Title: 19th century innovations : paving the way / Matthew McArdle.
Other titles: Ninetheenth century innovations
Description: Huntington Beach, CA : Teacher Created Materials, 2017. |
Includes index. | Audience: Grades 4-6.
Identifiers: LCCN 2016034140 (print) | LCCN 2016035396 (ebook) | ISBN
9781493837960 (pbk.) | ISBN 9781480757615 (eBook)
Subjects: LCSH: Technology--History--19th century--Juvenile literature. |
Inventions--History--19th century--Juvenile literature.
Classification: LCC T19 .M33 2017 (print) | LCC T19 (ebook) | DDC
609/.034--dc23
LC record available at https://lccn.loc.gov/2016034140

Teacher Created Materials
5301 Oceanus Drive
Huntington Beach, CA 92649-1030
http://www.tcmpub.com

ISBN 978-1-4938-3796-0

Printed by: 590835
Printed in: China

Table of Contents

A Century of Change 4

New Ways on the Water. 6

Path to the Pacific 12

Iron Horses 18

A Changing Way of Life 22

Dawn of a New Era 26

Code It! 28

Glossary 30

Index 31

Your Turn! 32

A Century of Change

The year is 1800. A 13-year-old girl named Jane has found work in a **factory** in Boston. She spins cotton into thread for hours each day. Jane uses her pay to support her family. As she walks home down a damp, lamp-lit street, Jane wonders how her life might change next. It already changed so much when she moved from the countryside to live in the city.

Jane was not alone. Sweeping changes came to the United States in the 1800s. More people moved to cities to work in factories. Many of them were women. Some of them earned money for the first time. More goods were produced and the **economy** improved. Furniture, farm tools, and other items were made faster than ever. New inventions, discoveries, and ideas transformed how people like Jane lived.

FIRST FACTORY

Samuel Slater built one of the first factories in the United States. He set up shop in Rhode Island in 1790. The workers turned cotton into cloth. Factories soon dotted the Northeast.

Boston, Massachusetts, in the early 1800s

New Ways on the Water

Around 1800, many Americans wanted to begin a new life. In the West, people could find plenty of land for farming. There was also much more room to raise a family.

The Ohio and Tennessee Valleys were filled with empty space. But settlers had to cross the Appalachian Mountains to get there. Getting past them was not easy. Many of the mountains were thousands of feet high. The journey was long and dangerous. Cadwallader Colden talked about digging a **canal**. Canals are man-made waterways. They allow boats to travel when rivers aren't deep enough. A canal would be an easier, faster way to get around the mountains.

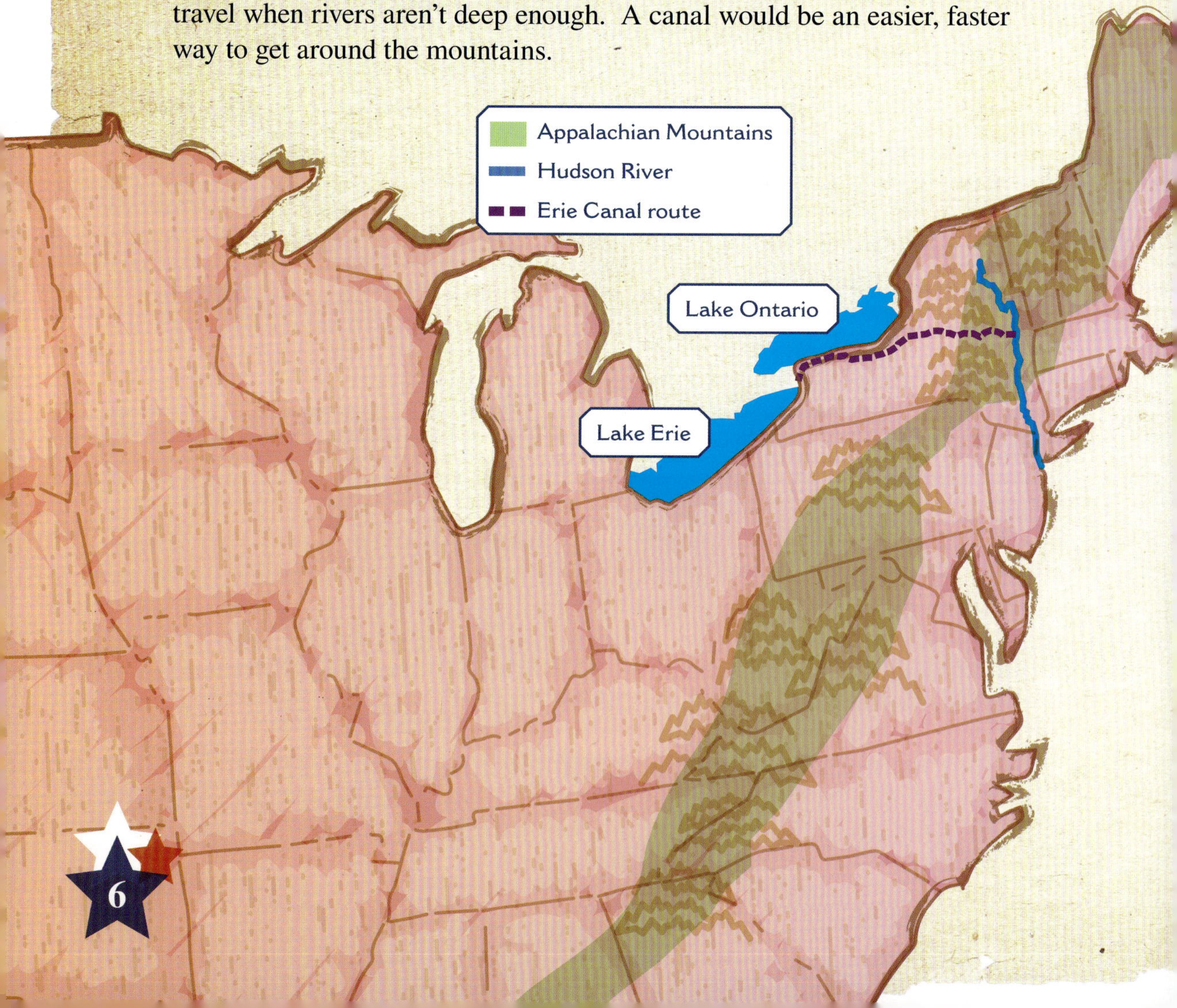

the Erie Canal in 1838

Colden was a land **surveyor**. He first suggested his canal idea in 1724. Colden wanted to build a canal to connect the Hudson River in New York with Lake Erie to the west. The canal would help settlers travel across the rugged landscape. Colden also thought the canal would increase trade between American Indians and Western settlers. The idea gained support as more people headed west. Soon, the Erie Canal would be built.

FATHER OF THE CANAL SYSTEM

Cadwallader Colden built the first canal in the United States near Montgomery, New York. But sadly, he did not live to see the Erie Canal completed. He died in 1776.

This 1846 painting of the Erie Canal shows all 10 completed locks.

LOCK SYSTEM

To pass through a lock, a boat moved between two gates. Both gates closed around the boat. Water poured into the lock until it reached the level of the water upstream. Then, the front gate opened and the boat passed through.

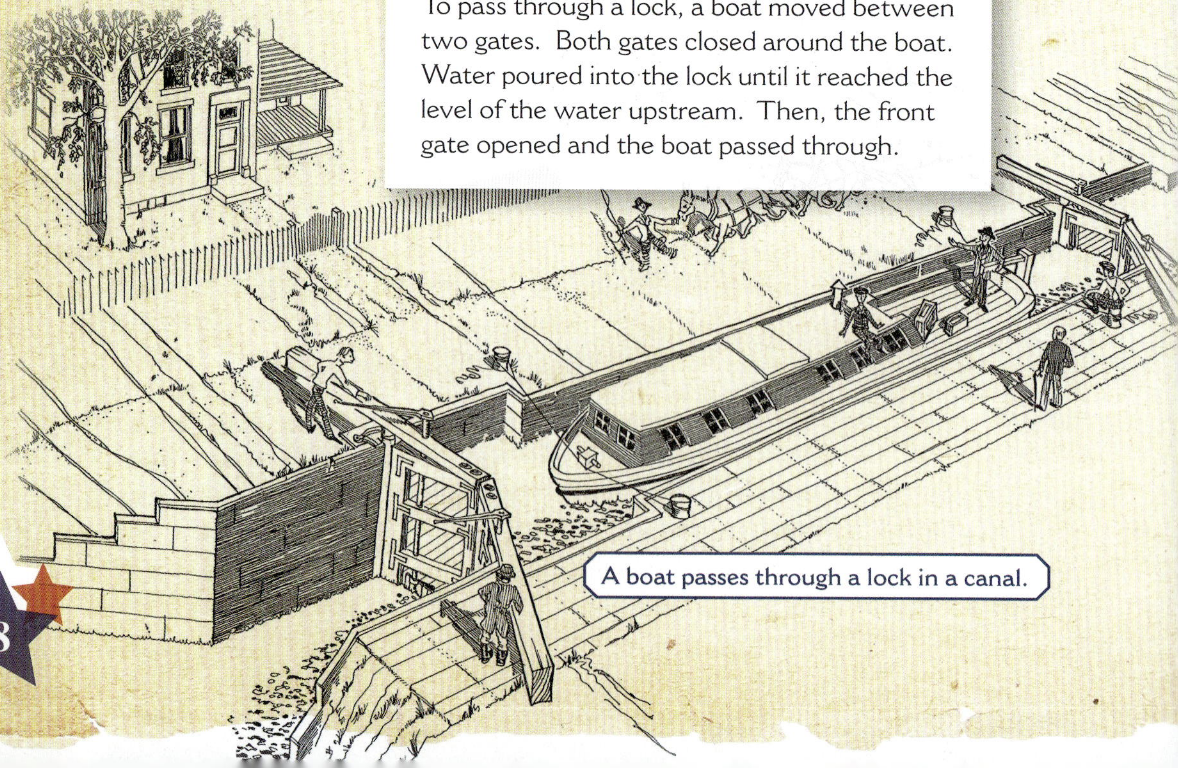

A boat passes through a lock in a canal.

Construction began in 1817. The work was grueling. Workers cut down forests and hauled away dirt. They worked long hours and earned very low wages. Many workers were bitten by mosquitoes and infected with malaria. At the time, this deadly disease was called *swamp fever.*

Lake Erie was more than 500 feet (152 meters) higher than the Hudson River. Workers had to find a way for boats to travel across different heights of land. They built **locks** that could raise and lower boats at certain points along the canal. Workers also had to build bridges so the canal could pass over rivers and hills. After 363 miles (584 kilometers) of digging, the canal was finished in 1825.

The Erie Canal was a huge success. As a result, more canals were built. The ability to ship goods along these waterways changed trade and travel across the country. Towns, such as Rochester and Buffalo, grew into bustling cities. By 1840, New York City was the nation's busiest **port**. Business was booming. These canals were soon filled with new types of boats to transport people and goods.

WEDDING OF THE WATERS

DeWitt Clinton, the governor of New York from 1811 to 1813, rode in the first boat that traveled the entire Erie Canal. Clinton poured water from Lake Erie into the Atlantic Ocean. People called it the "wedding of the waters."

People used many kinds of boats in the early 1800s. American Indians and fur trappers paddled canoes on streams. **Barges**, or flatboats, carried passengers and cargo. These boats were a common sight on lakes and rivers. People used sails, oars, and poles to move flatboats. Horses pulled other types of boats from roads alongside canals.

In 1807, Robert Fulton built the first commercial **steamboat**. This new type of boat harnessed the power of steam to move. Steamboats could easily move against the flow of water. People no longer needed to rely on horses, paddles, or the wind to move boats.

Robert Fulton's steamboat, *Clermont*

Robert Fulton

By the 1830s, steamboats were everywhere. They carried people up and down the Atlantic coast. They journeyed across the Erie Canal and throughout the Great Lakes. They traveled up the mighty Mississippi and Ohio Rivers. Steamboats transported cotton from the South and factory goods from the North. New Orleans grew into a major trading center. As the nation's waterways transformed, so did other modes of transportation.

WHAT MAKES A STEAM ENGINE?

To power a steam engine, coal is burned. The burning coal boils a tank of water, which turns to steam. The steam powers a piston that moves a paddlewheel, pushing the boat forward.

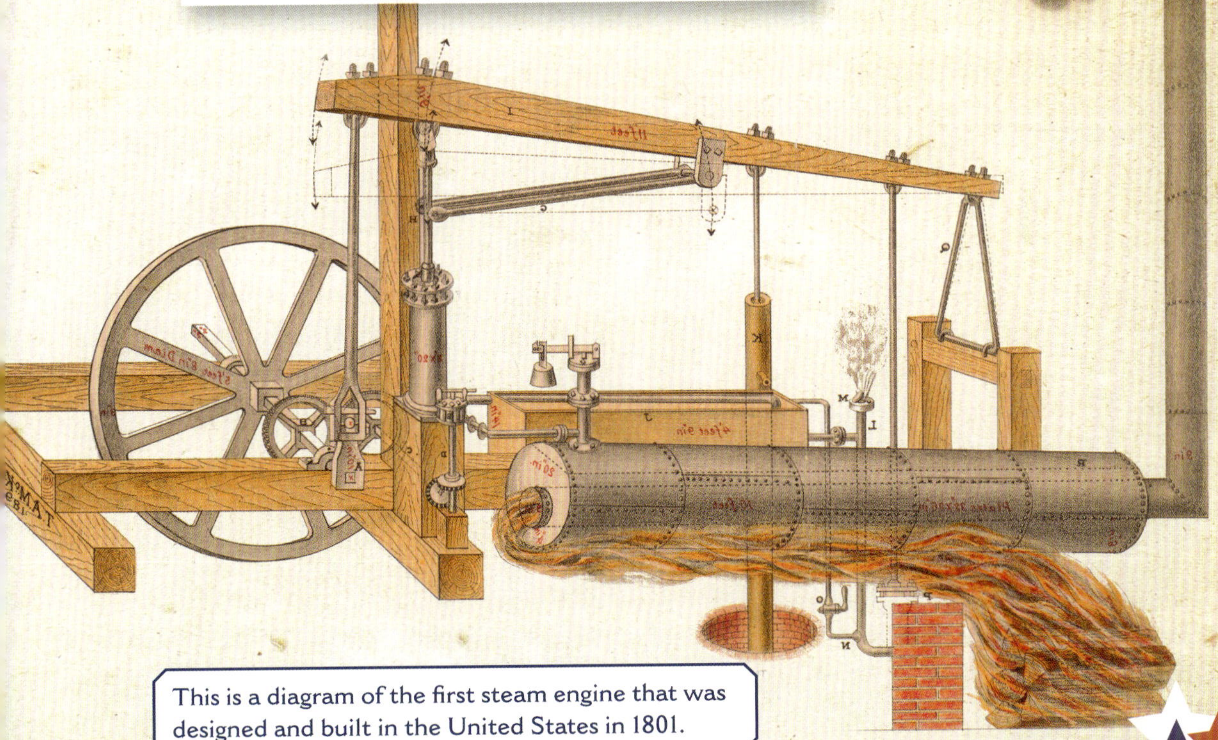

This is a diagram of the first steam engine that was designed and built in the United States in 1801.

Path to the Pacific

President Thomas Jefferson doubled the size of the country in 1803. This was the year that the United States purchased the Louisiana Territory from France. The nation now stretched to the Rocky Mountains. Settlers moved west to farm. But for many people, it was not enough. They believed the nation should reach all the way to the Pacific Ocean. This idea was called **Manifest Destiny**.

Manifest Destiny was one reason the United States went to war with Mexico in 1846. Settlers in Texas had broken away from Mexican rule and joined the United States. But the two nations did not agree where the border with Mexico was. The United States won the war. As a result, Mexico dropped its claim to Texas and handed over even more of its land for 15 million dollars. The new territory stretched all the way to California.

THIS LAND IS OURS

Many settlers took lands that belonged to Mexicans. The United States agreed to protect Mexicans living in the West after the war. But settlers often ignored this law. Many Mexicans lost everything.

Mexican and American forces battle in 1847.

Around this time, the nation also gained land in the Northwest. It was called the Oregon Territory. Suddenly, the country was huge. The nation got its wish. It now reached the Pacific Ocean. All this land offered more places where people could live. Thousands of settlers headed west to claim it. New **innovations** would soon follow.

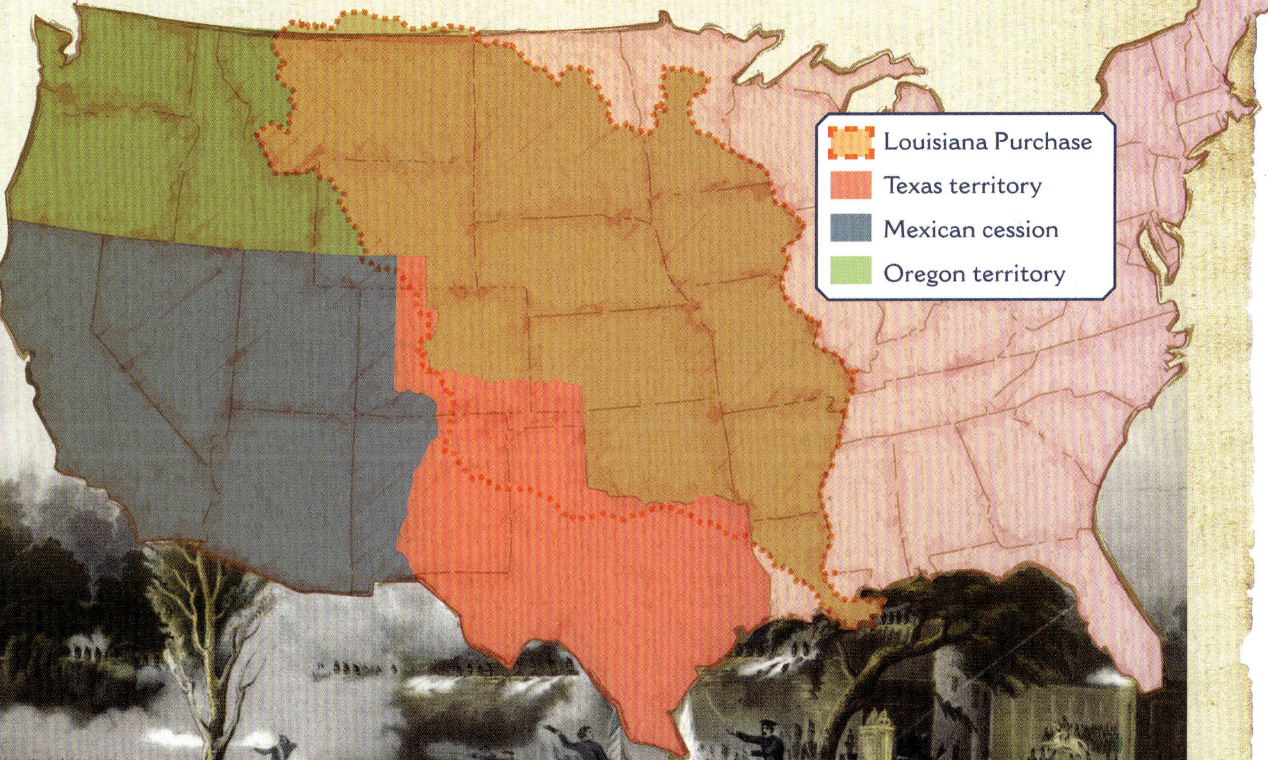

People journeyed west for many reasons. Millions of acres of land were up for grabs. Fish and game were plentiful. Gold was discovered in California in 1848. Eleven years later, silver was found in Nevada. The West became a place where people could get rich quickly. Thousands of poor factory workers, including women and children, lived in Eastern cities. They worked long hours for very low wages. For them, the **frontier** was a land of opportunity.

JUST PASSING THROUGH

James Beckwourth was a fur trapper and frontier guide in the West. He found a new way to cross the Sierra Nevada Mountains. The Beckwourth Pass made the journey to California much easier for thousands of settlers.

Miners in California search for gold and silver.

Pioneers head west in a wagon train.

Some people traveled west by ship. Ships sailed from the East Coast around the tip of South America. Then, they moved up the Pacific coast. This trip could take a whole year. Most people journeyed west in covered wagons pulled by horses or oxen. This only took four to six months. Settlers set off from Missouri on trails that stretched to Oregon and California. They often left in groups called **wagon trains.**

As the nation pushed west, people found themselves separated from their families by hundreds or thousands of miles. Since travel was so slow, people had to invent new ways to communicate over long distances.

A Pony Express rider reaches a station to change horses.

In California, San Francisco grew into a busy city. People from around the world settled there. But it could take months for mail to arrive by sea or by stagecoach. So, people came up with a faster way to deliver mail.

The Pony Express was that innovation. It delivered mail between California and Missouri. Young men on horses raced to pass mail between 190 stations. Riders switched every 75 to 100 mi. (120 to 160 km). Horses were changed every 10 to 15 mi. (16 to 24 km). They did this so the horses could run at top speeds. Now, mail could make the nearly 2,000-mile (3,200 km) trip in just 10 days. The service ran for more than a year.

In 1844, Samuel Morse developed a new **telegraph**. It used electricity to send messages called telegrams. Wires carried these messages over long distances. To send telegrams, Morse used dots and dashes to stand for letters. People called it *Morse code*. The sender typed out the Morse code. The receiver listened and changed the dots and dashes back into letters. The first telegraph line to stretch across the country was built in 1861. Sending messages was now lightning fast. As a result, the Pony Express shut down.

Samuel Morse

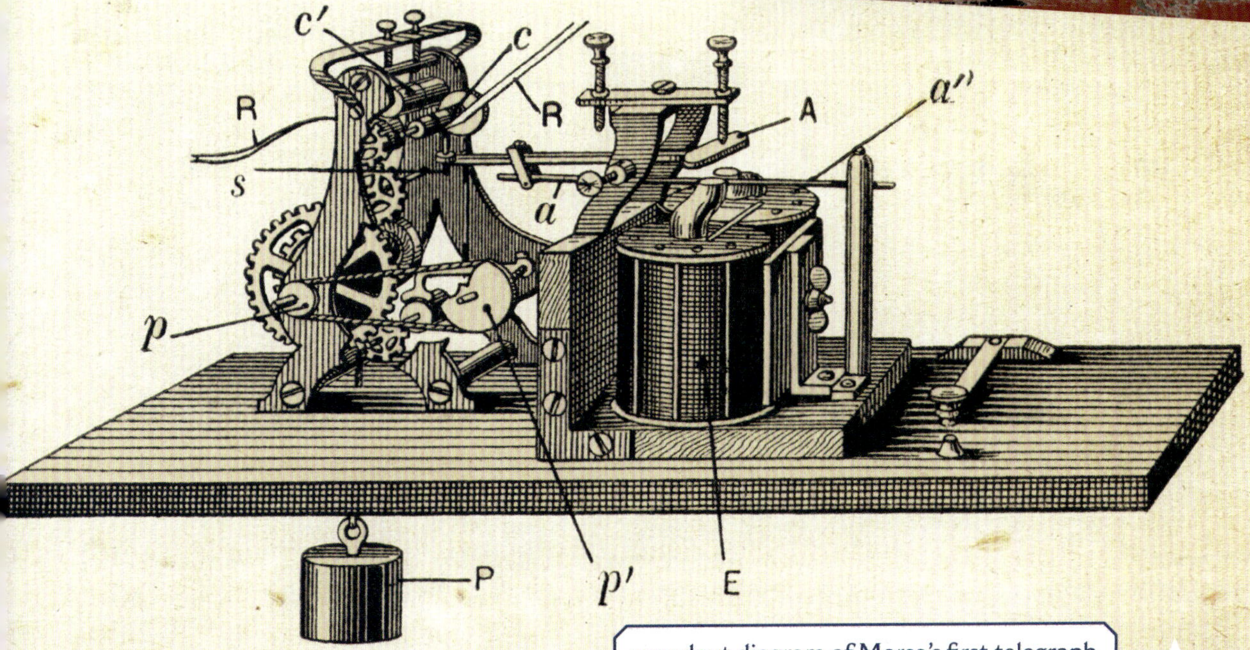

woodcut diagram of Morse's first telegraph

Iron Horses

As the years passed, people continued to innovate. They had to find a better way to transport all the goods and crops being produced around the country. Canals were expensive and difficult to build. Wagons were too slow. Another invention soon rattled and rolled onto the scene. The railroad became one of the most important achievements of its time.

Horses on steel tracks pulled the first trains. In 1825, John Stevens invented a train powered by steam. The first passenger steam train, or **locomotive**, in the nation set out in 1831. Locomotives soon dotted the landscape. People called them *iron horses*. Tracks were built all over the country, stretching to the edge of the frontier.

locomotive in 1861

A train and horse-drawn car race down the tracks.

Railroads played a major role during the Civil War. A strong railroad system allowed the North to quickly move supplies and troops. The South had fewer railroads. It couldn't compete, giving a huge advantage to the North.

In 1862, President Abraham Lincoln signed a law that changed the country. The law called for two companies to build a **transcontinental** railroad. One company would build west from the Missouri River. The other would build east from California.

EXPLODING TRAINS

Early locomotives earned terrible marks for safety. They sometimes shot sparks, jumped their tracks, or even exploded. New train designs included headlights and better smokestacks.

Construction started in 1863 as the Civil War raged. Workers were hard to find. When the war ended, former soldiers headed west looking for work. So did newly freed African Americans. The rail companies hired them. In California, Chinese, German, and Irish **immigrants** joined the rail crews. Building the railroads was a team effort.

The golden spike is driven into the ground.

A SHAMEFUL POLICY

Chinese immigrants helped build the transcontinental railroad. Some people blamed them for taking jobs. So in 1882, the government stopped Chinese immigrants from coming to the United States. Many years passed before the law was changed.

The work was dangerous. Workers built bridges over rivers and filled deep canyons. They blasted through solid rock as they tunneled through mountains. Many people died during construction. But in 1869, the tracks finally came together in Utah. A golden spike was driven into the ground to celebrate.

Less than a week after the new railroad was finished, it opened to passengers. Traveling across the country now took only a few days. On a wagon, the journey took months. Goods from the East could be easily shipped to every part of the frontier. Western crops were sent east. By the 1880s, travelers could choose between several railroad lines. In 1890, so many people had settled in the West that the government said the frontier no longer existed.

A Changing Way of Life

New inventions continued to improve how people lived. The American way of life was changing.

Richard March Hoe built a faster printing press in 1847. It could print newspapers at a rate of 8,000 pages per hour. Hoe kept improving his printing press. By 1870, he could print 18,000 double-sided sheets per hour. This made printing cheaper and faster. Newspapers were printed in cities across the country.

Elisha Graves Otis invented a safety brake for elevators in 1852. Now, people could safely travel up and down tall buildings. As a result, huge buildings with steel frames were built. The Home Insurance Building in Chicago was the nation's first skyscraper. It reached a height of 138 ft. (42 m) and stood 10 stories tall.

When Josephine Cochrane's husband died in 1883, she was left in debt. Poor and alone, Cochrane built the first dishwasher. But it wasn't getting noticed. Then, in 1893, it won first place at an exhibition. Soon, dishwashers were in many homes and hotels.

the Home Insurance Building in Chicago, completed in 1885

a demonstration of the Hoe printing press in 1876

PAVING THE WAY

In 1790, women won the right to file for **patents**. But since women still couldn't own property in most states, many women didn't see the point in filing. On May 5, 1809, Mary Kies changed that. She became the first woman in the United States to successfully file a patent for her method of weaving straw with silk to make hats.

Mary Kies

Alexander Graham Bell makes the first long-distance telephone call on October 18, 1892.

In 1876, Alexander Graham Bell invented the telephone. This forever changed the way people communicated. A device at one end of the line changed the sounds of people's voices into electrical signals. These signals passed through a wire. At the other end of the line, the signals were changed back into sound. Soon, telephone lines stretched across the country. People hundreds of miles apart could hear each other's voices.

CREDIT WHERE CREDIT IS DUE

In 1868, Margaret Knight invented a machine that created square-bottomed bags. Knight filed for a patent but learned that a rival inventor had stolen her idea and filed his own patent. Knight sued and won. Over her lifetime, Knight would be granted 26 more patents.

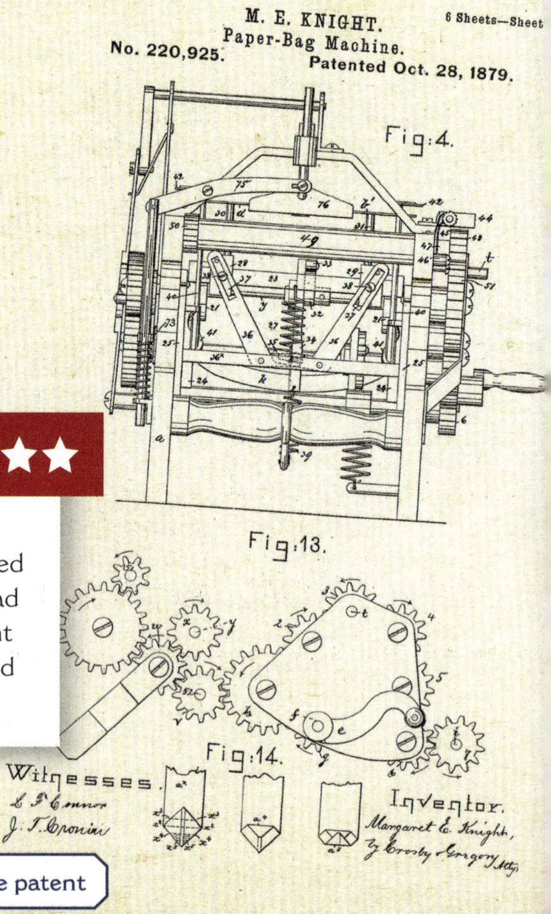

Knight's paper bag machine patent

Thomas Edison was another inventor. He invented many things. After hundreds of attempts, Edison perfected the light bulb in 1879. This was his masterpiece. It transformed how people lived. Using electricity, the bulb could produce light at the flick of a switch.

In 1882, Edison and his team built the first permanent power station in New York City. The station had wires, meters, and **generators**. The generators produced electricity to light the city. Homes lit up. Dark streets became much safer. Shops filled with people, and businesses grew. Oil lamps were no longer needed. Other cities around the country soon put up lights, too. The nation never looked back.

Thomas Edison

Dawn of a New Era

It is now the year 1900. It's been a mere 100 years since a young girl named Jane arrived in Boston. In her old footsteps walks a 13-year-old boy named Henry. He is visiting Boston for the first time. Lights glow everywhere around him. Tall buildings tower overhead. He rides an elevator to the top floor of one of them and gazes out at the city. Homes and other buildings stretch far into the distance. Henry thinks back to his great-grandmother Jane and wonders if she felt the same excitement he does.

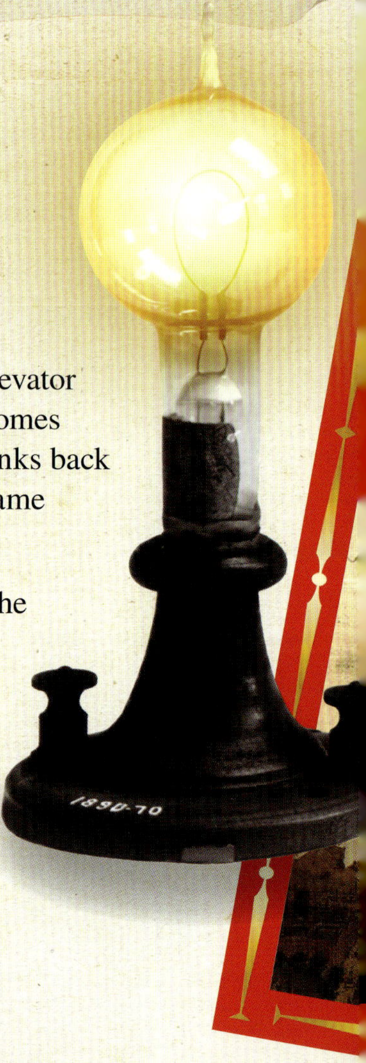

The United States secured its place as a world power. The country was stronger than ever. The spirit of innovation that helped the nation blossom continued to grow. The next hundred years would bring even more changes. But the same optimism that inspired settlers, inventors, writers, and others to strive for a better life was in full swing. The American Dream was here to stay.

Copley Square, Boston, Massachusetts in the early 20th century

Boston, Massachusetts in the late 1800s

Code It!

Morse code changed the way people sent messages across the frontier. Telegraphs made communication faster than ever before.

Imagine you are a settler in the 1800s who just reached California. Write a short telegram to your family back east describing your journey. Use Morse code to write your letter. Be sure to leave plenty of space between words. Once you're finished, trade your letter with a partner. Then, decode each other's letters.

Glossary

barges—large, flat-bottomed boats that carry goods and people on waterways

canal—a waterway dug across land used for the passage of goods and people

economy—the system of buying and selling goods and services

factory—a building where products are made

frontier—an area where few people live

generators—machines that produce electrical energy

immigrants—people who come to a country to live there

innovations—new ideas, inventions, discoveries, or processes

locks—areas that raise and lower boats in canals using gates to control the flow of water

locomotive—a train powered by a steam engine

Manifest Destiny—the idea that the United States had a right to extend its borders to the Pacific Ocean

patents—documents that give a person or company the right to be the only one that makes or sells a certain product

port—a harbor where ships pick up and drop off goods

steamboat—a boat powered by a steam engine

surveyor—a person who measures and inspects an area of land

telegraph—an old-fashioned system of sending messages over long distances using wires and electrical signals

transcontinental—spanning across a continent

wagon trains—groups of wagons traveling in single-file lines to distant lands

Index

African Americans, 20
American Dream, 26
American Indians, 7, 10
Beckwourth, James, 14
Bell, Alexander Graham, 24
Chinese immigrants, 20–21
Clinton, DeWitt, 9
Cochrane, Josephine, 22
Colden, Cadwallader, 6–7
Edison, Thomas, 25
Fulton, Robert, 10
German immigrants, 20
Hoe, Richard March, 22
Irish immigrants, 20
Jefferson, Thomas, 12
Kies, Mary, 23
Knight, Margaret, 24
Lincoln, Abraham, 19
Mexico, 12
Morse, Samuel, 17
Otis, Elisha Graves, 22
Pony Express, 16–17
Slater, Samuel, 4
Stevens, John, 18

Your Turn!

New Innovations

There were many new innovations in the 1800s that changed the way people lived. What innovation or invention do you think was the most important? Create an ad for it. Use language and pictures to convince people in the 1800s that they should buy or use this invention or innovation.